The North American Third Edition

Cambridge Latin Course
Unit 2   Workbook

Revision Editor
Ed Phinney
Chair, Department of Classics, & Director, University Foreign Language Resource
University of Massachusetts at Amherst, U.S.A.

Consulting Editor
Patricia E. Bell
Teacher of Latin & Assistant Head of Languages
Centennial Collegiate and Vocational Institute, Guelph, Ontario, Canada

Editorial Assistant
Barbara Romaine
Amherst, Massachusetts, U.S.A.

CAMBRIDGE
UNIVERSITY PRESS

Guidelines

We have produced this workbook, like the workbook for Unit 1, for junior high school and high school students using the North American Third Edition of the Cambridge Latin Course. The workbook provides reinforcement exercises additional to those already contained in the students' textbook. Because the exercises are supplementary and optional, students should work them after they have completed both the stories and the "Practicing the Language" drills in the textbook.

If students, while working the exercises, do not recognize the ending of an inflected Latin word or are puzzled by the structure of a Latin sentence, they should consult the relevant section in the Unit 2 Review Grammar, pp. 162–89. If they do not know the English meaning of a Latin word, they should look up the Latin word in the Unit 2 Complete Vocabulary, pp. 198–213.

You will find diagnostic tests for students in the Unit 2 Teacher's Manual, pp. 100–104, and may obtain master copies of the annual Unit Examinations for the Cambridge Latin Course (produced by the North American Cambridge Classics Project) by writing to the Resource Center, North American Cambridge Classics Project (NACCP), Box 932, Amherst, MA. 01004–0932 U.S.A.

Stage 13

13.1 What does he or she want to do?

Circle the Latin words in parentheses which describe the action of the character in each picture.

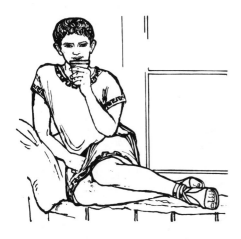

1 Quīntus (pecūniam numerāre / vīnum bibere) vult.

2 Grumiō (cēnam gustāre / statuam facere) vult.

3 Cerberus (in viā dormīre / vīllam custōdīre) vult.

4 Metella (barbam tondēre / ātrium īnspicere) vult.

Continued

5 mercātor (togās vēndere / fēminās vituperāre) vult.

6 Clēmēns hospitibus (vīnum offerre / fābulam nārrāre) vult.

7 Celer (servum emere / leōnem pingere) vult.

8 servus (dormīre / labōrāre) vult.

9 Volūbilis (cēnam coquere / horreum aedificāre) vult.

10 canis (cervum invenīre / epistulam scrībere) vult.

13.2 What can she, he, or it do?

In each answer, circle the correct Latin word(s).

1 *Question:* potestne versipellis fābulam mīrābilem nārrāre?
   Answer: versipellis fābulam mīrābilem nārrāre (potest /
   nōn potest).

2 *Question:* potestne canis vīllam cūrāre?
   Can a dog take care of a house?
   Answer: canis vīllam cūrāre (potest / nōn potest).

3 *Question:* potestne Quīntus vīnum bibere?
   Can Quintus drink wine?
   Answer: Quīntus vīnum bibere (potest / nōn potest).

4 *Question:* potestne nauta in triclīniō nāvigāre?
   Can a sailor sail in a triclinium?
   Answer: nauta in triclīniō nāvigāre (potest / nōn potest).

5 *Question:* potestne fūr īnfantem parvum tacitē ē vīllā portāre?
   Can a thief carry a small baby silently from a house?
   Answer: fūr parvum īnfantem tacitē ē vīllā portāre (potest / nōn potest).

6 *Question:* potestne Anti-Loquāx suāviter cantāre?
   Answer: Anti-Loquāx suāviter cantāre
   (potest / nōn potest).

13.3 What can you do?

In each answer, fill the correct set of blanks with "**possum**" or "**nōn possum**."

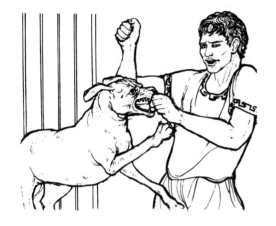

1 *Question:* potesne tū canem ferōcem pulsāre?
  Can you hit a fierce dog?
  Answer: ego canem ferōcem pulsāre

  (— — — — — —).

  (— — — — — — — — —).

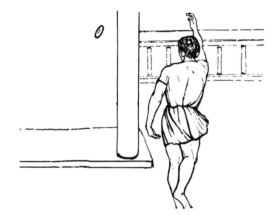

2 *Question:* potesne tū discum longē ēmittere?
  Can you throw a discus a long way?
  Answer: ego discum longē ēmittere

  (— — — — — —).

  (— — — — — — — — —).

3 *Question:* potesne tū suāviter cantāre?
  Answer: ego suāviter cantāre

  (— — — — — —).

  (— — — — — — — — —).

4 *Question:* potesne tū horreum aedificāre?
Answer: ego horreum aedificāre

(— — — — — —).

(— — —   — — — — — —).

5 *Question:* potesne tū in mēnsam salīre?
Answer: ego in mēnsam salīre

(— — — — — —).

(— — —   — — — — — —).

6 *Question:* potesne tū optimē saltāre?
Answer: ego optimē saltāre

(— — — — — —).

(— — —   — — — — — —).

7 *Question:* potesne tū pictūram splendidam pingere?
Answer: ego pictūram splendidam pingere

(— — — — — —).

(— — —   — — — — — —).

8 *Question:* potesne tū statuam facere?
Answer: ego statuam facere

(— — — — — —).

(— — —   — — — — — —).

9 *Question:* potesne tū cēnam optimam coquere?
Answer: ego cēnam optimam coquere

(— — — — — —).

(— — —   — — — — — —).

10 *Question:* potesne tū celeriter currere?
Answer: ego celeriter currere

(— — — — — —).

(— — —   — — — — — —).

13.4 A Romano-British Farm

Study the picture below, and then answer the questions.

1 From where did the family of the house get water for their animals?

2 How did the farmer's wife sweeten the family's boiled cereal? How do **you** sweeten your cereal?

3 What animals pulled the farmer's plow? (Hint: look at the photograph in your Unit 2 textbook, p.13.)

4 What other object in the picture might these animals also have pulled?

5 What grain-crops might the farmer have grown in the field he is plowing? (Hint: consult your Unit 2 textbook, p.17.)

6 Which of the grain-crops you listed in Question 5 do **you** eat? In what dishes do you eat them? Which do you like best?

7 Study the drawings of ancient farm tools in your Unit 2 textbook, p.17; copy the drawings below and label each tool with its correct name. Choose names from the following list: sickle / two-bladed hoe / spade.

8 Study this drawing of a Roman plow. What do you think was the purpose of the colter? (Hint: look up *culter* in a Latin dictionary.)

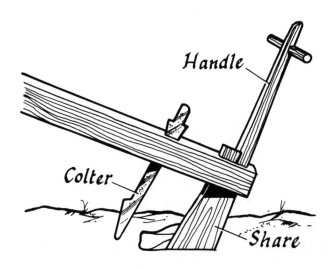

Handle

Colter

Share

13.5 The Slaves on Salvius' Farm

1 Study the pictures below with their captions.

Bregāns cum multīs servīs labōrat.

Cervīx arātōrēs īnspicit.

Salvius in vīllā magnificā habitat.

Vārica est vīlicus. vīllam et servōs cūrat.

2 After the Romans invaded Britain and established a province, which of the men above was sent by the emperor to supervise law and order in the south? Put his name in Box 2 below.

| 1 Emperor | → | 2 | → | 3 | → | 4 | → | 5 |

Then fill in the names of the other men pictured above in order of status.

13.6 Romano-British Iron Mines

When, after A.D. 43, the Romans gradually increased their control of tribal Britain, they took over the country's mines of gold, silver, lead, tin, copper and iron. But they imposed the drudgery of the actual mining on slaves who were often chained together into gangs with the neck-cuffs shown in the Unit 2 textbook, p.6.

Iron was particularly important to the soldiers in the Roman army of occupation, since they needed iron to repair or replace their equipment. Thus when the special commissioner Salvius, in the story "coniūrātiō" (Unit 2, pp.6–7), is imagined as having visited what is now the county of Kent to inspect a new iron mine, he makes sure every slave-worker is healthy and able to work hard. He has the one slave he finds sick executed.

Many of the iron mines which the Romans took were in the territory of the Cantiaci tribe, now Kent. Part of Kent and the area reaching westward into modern East Sussex is known as the "Weald," or woodland, because of the forests which once covered it. The trees were cut to provide fuel (charcoal) for the iron-smelting furnaces which continued to be an important industry there until about 300 years ago.

1   Copy, on a separate sheet of paper, the map of Roman Britain in the Unit 2 textbook, p.38. After consulting a map of modern Britain, draw in the boundaries of the modern counties of Kent, and of East and West Sussex.

2   On a map of modern Britain, find the village of Angmering-on-Sea (just west of the city of Worthing, in the county of West Sussex). Here was located the country villa which Salvius owned. Mark the place on your map with a dot and label it Angmering/Salvius' villa.

Notice how close Salvius lived to the Weald and its iron mines.

Continued

This Roman-period tombstone, found in Northern England, shows the deceased, a blacksmith, as he appeared in real life. The blacksmith works at his anvil and pounds a piece of red-hot iron (held by tongs) with the hammer in his right hand. Notice his protective apron, the top of which runs diagonally across his hips.

The piece of iron which the blacksmith pounds began as ore from a mine. In Roman times, iron ore was often close to the surface and therefore easily loosened with pickaxes and then gathered up. Near to a source of ore would have been one or more furnaces for reducing it to hard iron. One such furnace is shown below. Study the picture:

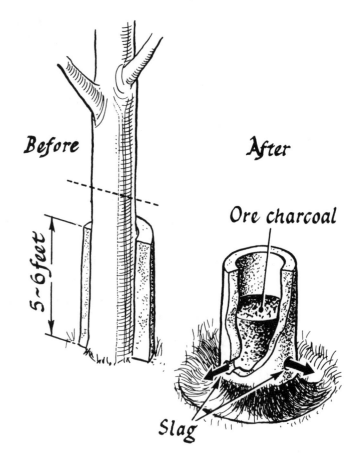

Before   *After*

Ore charcoal

5~6 feet

Slag

The tubular shaft-furnace (shown above, at right, in a vertical cross section) was made of clay, which had been plastered in layers around a tree-trunk and successively baked, till hard, by wood fires heaped around the bottom of the plastered tree-trunk. Eventually, the heat of the fires would have reduced, or "calcined," the tree-trunk to ashes, which could then be removed, leaving the hard-baked, clay shell to be used as a "smelting" furnace.

The sides of the shaft-furnace were about a foot (30cm) thick and five to six feet (1.5–2 meters) high. Workers packed iron ore and charcoal inside the shaft to a height of two feet (60cm), leaving the rest of the shaft to serve as a chimney. They lighted the charcoal and then, with a bellows, pumped air in through an opening near the bottom to keep the charcoal burning.

As the fire raged at a temperature as high as 2400°F (=1300°C), a glassy material, called "slag," poured out through low slits into adjoining pits. Finally, a lump of iron, called the "bloom," was left inside the furnace. When it was cool, workers lifted the lump through the top of the shaft with long tongs. Later, blacksmiths like the one pictured on the tombstone opposite worked the iron-lump into swords or spears, sickles or colters, axes or hammers, hinges or locks, keys or nails, etc.

1   Look up in a large English dictionary the following mining terms: *calcining, ore, reduction, smelting, slag, slag-tap furnace, slagging hole, slagman, bloom, wrought iron*. On your paper, make a glossary of the words and their meanings but write the meanings in your own words.

2   Look up in an encyclopedia *charcoal*, probably a sub-heading under *carbon*, and study the description of the process by which charcoal is manufactured. Find a diagram showing a kiln for making charcoal. Then on your paper, copy the diagram and write a description of the process in your own words.

3   Visit your school's artroom and ask the teacher to show you a charcoal drawing, a charcoal pencil, and a tube of charcoal-black pigment. Do you know any other modern uses for charcoal?

Stage 14

14.1 The Slaves in Salvius' Rural House

1 Study the pictures below with their titles. They show three slaves from the household of Salvius and Rufilla.

Domitilla est ōrnātrīx.

Philus in tablīnō labōrat.

Marcia pavīmentum lavat.

2 Answer the questions below.

1 Which TWO slaves would have had a higher status, and why?

_____ and _____ would have had a higher status than _____

because _____

_____

2 What is Philus using, and what is it for?

_____

14.2 Is it necessary or not?

1 Read each of the following questions and then answer by writing "**necesse est mihi**" or "**nōn necesse est mihi**" in the appropriate blank.

1 *Question:* necesse est tibi hodiē dōnum emere?

   Answer: _____

2 *Question:* necesse est tibi hodiē canem cūrāre?

   Answer: _____

3 *Question:* necesse est tibi hodiē familiārem vīsitāre?

   Answer: _____

4 *Question:* necesse est tibi hodiē librum legere?

   Answer: _____

5 *Question:* necesse est tibi hodiē pāvōnem cōnsūmere?

   Answer: _____

6 *Question:* necesse est tibi hodiē vīnum bibere?

   Answer: _____

7 *Question:* necesse est tibi linguam Latīnam discere?

   Answer: _____

2 Explain in your own words the reasons for each answer above.

14.3 Is the nominative a singular or plural?

In each Latin sentence, circle the Latin adjective in parentheses which matches its noun.

1 How many *small boys* are there?
sunt duo puerī (parvus / parvī).

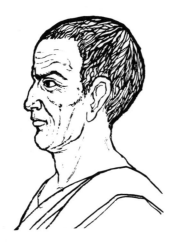

2 How many *cruel Romans* are there?
est ūnus Rōmānus (crūdēlēs / crūdēlis).

3 How many *full wine-jars* are there?
sunt novem amphorae (plēnae / plēna).

4 How many *lazy slaves* are there?
sunt trēs servī (ignāvus / ignāvī).

5 How many *bronze jugs* are there?
est ūna urna (aēnea / aēneae).

6 How many *silver tripods* are there?
sunt duo tripodes (argenteī / argenteus).

If the above exercise is too hard, study again the Unit 2 textbook, p.27, ¶¶ 4–6, and / or the Unit 2 Review Grammar pp. 167–68.

14.4 Is the accusative a singular or plural?

In each Latin sentence, circle the Latin adjective in parentheses which matches its noun.

1 How many *faithful slaves* is Salvius supervising?
Salvius quīnque servōs (fidēlem / fidēlēs) cūrat.

2 How many *busy slave-girls* is Rufilla supervising?
Rūfilla trēs ancillās (occupātās / occupātam) cūrat.

3 How many *big dogs* is Bregans neglecting?
Bregāns duōs canēs (magnum / magnōs) nōn cūrat.

4   How many *heavy wine-jars* are the twins holding?
geminī ūnam amphoram (gravēs / gravem) tenent.

5   How many *huge wine-jars* is Bregans looking at?
Bregāns trēs amphorās (ingentem / ingentēs) spectat.

6   How many *wine-jars* is Varica pointing out?
Vārica (ūnam/duās) amphoram dēmōnstrat?

14.5 Philus miser

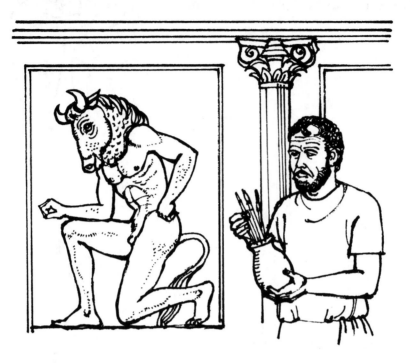

Read the following story, and then write the answers to the questions in the space opposite.

Philus erat miser, quod per tōtum diem labōrāvit.
  "quam fessus sum!" inquit. "semper necesse est mihi numerāre.
'numerā amphorās!' dīcit Vārica. 'numerā togās!' dīcit Rūfilla. 'numerā
servōs!' dīcit Salvius. 'numerā! numerā!' semper audiō. et nunc necesse
est mihi multōs dēnāriōs in tablīnō numerāre. nōnne miserrimus sum?"   5
  Philus, postquam tablīnum intrāvit, pictūram vīdit. Philus pictūram
īnspexit, quod pictūra nova erat. in pictūrā erat <u>Mīnōtaurus,</u> mōnstrum
ferōcissimum.
  subitō Philus <u>pēnicillum</u> rapuit et in Mīnōtaurō "SALVIUS" scrīpsit.
tum, quod ibi manēre et dēnāriōs numerāre nōlēbat, ē tablīnō festīnāvit.   10
  Salvius et amīcī mox tablīnum intrāvērunt. amīcī erant mercātōrēs
Rōmānī. Salvius amīcīs pictūram novam dēmōnstrāvit. amīcī, ubi
pictūram vīdērunt, rīsērunt.
  "cūr rīdētis?" rogāvit Salvius.
  "pictūra est optima," respondērunt amīcī.   15
  et Salvius rīsit quod erat <u>myops</u>.

Mīnōtaurus   *Minotaur (= taurus "bull" of King Minos), a mythical monster*
pēnicillum: pēnicillus *paint-brush*
myops   *shortsighted*

1 Why was Philus tired?

2 Why did he go into Salvius' study?

3 What did he see there?

4 What did he do then?

5 Why didn't Salvius notice what Philus had done?

6 Why do you think that the modern antibiotic-drug "penicillin" was named after the ancient *penicillus?* (Hint: look up in a large English dictionary "penicillium.")

7 In a handbook of Classical mythology, read the myth of Theseus and the Minotaur. Write out the story in your own words. Who were the parents of the Minotaur? Why was he half-bull? Why was he called "Mino-taur"? What and where was the Labyrinth? Who built the Labyrinth? Do you think Philus may have felt he too was trapped in a labyrinth? Why?

Stage 15

15.1 Describe the picture

Circle the correct Latin word(s) in parentheses, and then write the answer to the question with a full English sentence.

1 vidēsne (rhētorem / mercātōrem), quī trēs (puerōs / puellās) docet?

(I see) _____

2 vidēsne (templum / plaustrum), quod (in viā / in vīllā) iacet?

(I see) _____

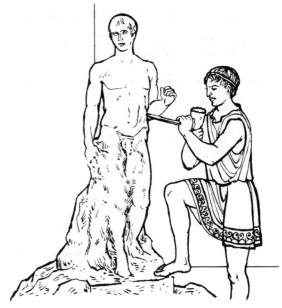

3 vidēsne (sculptōrem / pictōrem), quī (fābulam / statuam) facit?

(I see) _____

4 vidēsne (dominam / ancillam), quae (urnam / aulam) portat?

(I see) _____

5 vidēsne (servum / dominum), quī (taurum / agnum) dūcit?

(I see) _____

15.2 Complē hoc plaustrum!

Fill the squares in the wagon below with Latin words which translate the English (some hints are provided in parentheses).

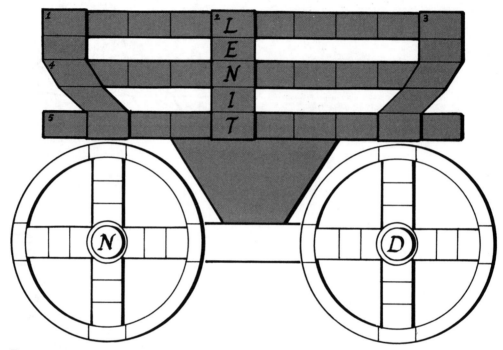

Across

1 as soon as
4 to leave (behind) (related to English *relic* and *relinquish*)
5 hairdressers

Down

1 sister (related to English *sorority* or French *sœur*)
2 *lēnit* = "she soothes"
3 to buy

The wheels (All words radiate outward from hub.)

First wheel
(a) nine
(b) I tell
(c) nothing
(d) cloud

Second wheel
(a) you (sg.) ought
(b) gift
(c) I dictate
(d) she gave

15.3 Roman Possessions

1 All these objects might have been found in or around a Roman country villa.

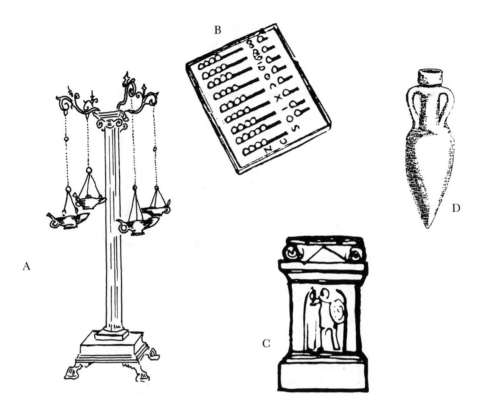

What are they? Put the correct letter in the box by each word.

ārā ☐   abacus ☐   candēlābrum ☐   amphora ☐

2 Choose **two** of these objects and describe **one** thing about each (e.g. who used it, what it was made of, how it was used).

_____

_____

_____

_____

15.4 Procession to King Cogidubnus' Palace

Re-read lines 1–7 of "ad aulam" in your Unit 2 textbook, Stage 15, pp. 46–47, and then follow the instructions below.

1 Match the object(s) in each box with the name of the person(s) who carried it or them in the procession. Write the letter of the appropriate person(s) in the blank under each object.

 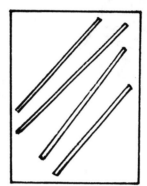 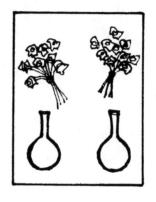 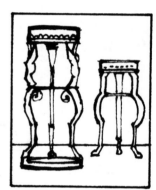

——————   ——————   ——————   ——————

A praecursōrēs   **C** servus
B ancilla   **D** aliae ancillae

2 How many people were there in the procession? *Circle the correct answer below.*

1–10   11–20   over 20

3 How many animals were there in the procession? *Circle the correct answer below.*

2   3   10

4 Circle the correct Latin words and make a Latin sentence which means the same as the English.

The ten forerunners who were going in front held sticks.

| quīnque | praecursor | quī | in prīmā parte | ībant | virgās | tenēbant. |
| decem | praecursōrēs | quem | in mediā parte | ībat | virgam | tenēbat. |

26

15.5 Roman Sites, Roads, and British Tribes

Match the following names with the numbers on the map below by writing the correct number in each blank. (You may, if necessary, consult the map in your Unit 2 textbook, p.38, and compare it with a map of modern Britain.)

_____ Wroxeter   _____ Fosse Way

_____ Regnenses tribe (Sussex)   _____ Exeter

_____ London   _____ York

_____ Watling Street   _____ Lincoln

_____ Cantiaci tribe (Kent)   _____ Colchester

15.6 The Emperor Claudius Invades Britain, A.D. 43

The general Julius Caesar crossed over twice to Britain with an army (in 55 and 54 B.C.), but returned to Rome without annexing the island. Over 90 years later, the Emperor Caligula (reigned A.D. 37–41) drew up a large army along the shore of "Oceanus," the ocean which washed the shore of western Europe. Because Oceanus, like a moat, shielded Europe from outlying, mysterious islands like Britain, Caligula (who was perhaps insane) became too frightened to cross; instead he told his soldiers to collect seashells from the beach and pretend, after returning to Rome, that they had seized them from Oceanus by force. Many Romans, particularly those who had never seen Oceanus, believed the ocean was also a mighty god.

Braver travelers, according to the Roman geographer Strabo, had reported that the island was rich in minerals, grain, animal hides, and hunting dogs. The weather in winter was more often rainy than snowy. The Britons themselves tended to be blonder and taller than the Romans. They were mostly nomadic, cutting a clearing in the forest for their huts and cattle-corrals and then in a few years moving on.

Claudius, after succeeding Caligula as emperor, decided that the time had come for the final effective invasion of Britain. Three divisions of soldiers landed ahead of him and while marching northward, won several battles against the combined forces of some native tribes. When the Romans reached the Thames river, their field commander set up camp and sent for the emperor. Claudius was ready in Rome, waiting with a large contingent of crack troops and even, according to one historian, a detachment of war-elephants.

The Emperor Claudius set out with his forces, reached and crossed (with or without the elephants) the dreaded Oceanus, and joined the advance army at the Thames. When he had taken command of all the forces, he crossed the river, met and defeated the last resisting Britons, and went on to capture Camulodunum, a center of tribal resistance.

A bronze head of the Emperor Claudius.

About Claudius' Invasion

Below is an outline map of western Europe, with certain rivers marked with their modern names. Study a complete, modern map of western Europe and then put labels on the outline map as instructed.

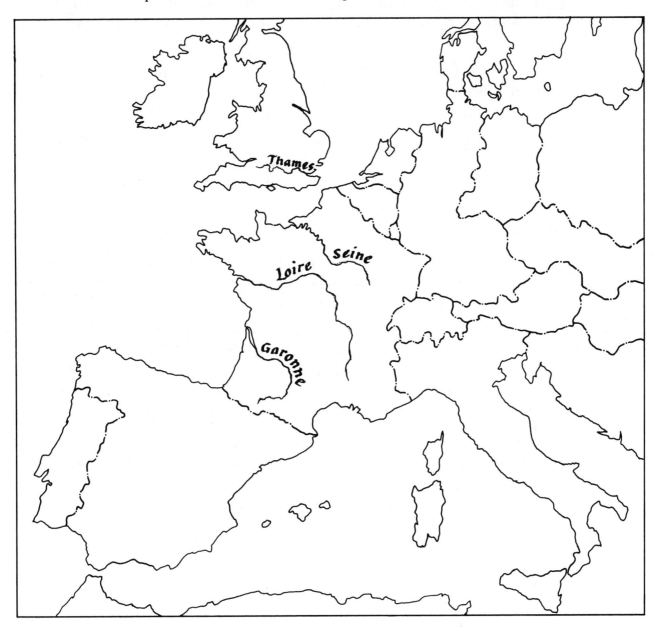

1 On the modern map, find the locations of the modern countries of Italy, France, and Britain (ancient *Ītalia*, *Gallia*, and *Britannia*).
   Label the three countries on the outline map with large block letters.

2 Find the city of Rome and its ancient harbor Ostia, from where Claudius set sail for Britain.
   With dots, mark their locations on the outline map and label them.

Continued

3 Find the modern names of what was believed by the Emperor Claudius to be part of Oceanus: (1) the narrow body of water stretching between Boulogne and, on the English side, Dover, and (2) the wider body of water between southern England and northern France.

Write the modern names of these bodies of water to the left of the outline map, and then draw arrows from the names to their appropriate locations on the map.

4 Find the site of Richborough (ancient *Rutupiae*), where the fleet of Claudius landed in Britain. (Hint: it is near the town of Sandwich, in Kent.)

With a dot, mark its location on the outline map and label it.

5 Find the modern town of Colchester (ancient *Camulodūnum*), where Claudius established the first capital of Britain.

With a dot, mark its location on the outline map and label it.

Additional Projects

1 Consult the appropriate section of an encyclopedia or Roman history book, and then describe why the Emperor Claudius wanted to invade Britain. What was the reputation of Britain? What was the reputation of Claudius? Why did he go ahead with the invasion?

2 Look up the legends of Hercules and Ulysses in a handbook of Classical mythology. Find and study the episodes in which these heroes crossed Oceanus in unusual boats. In what kind of boat did Ulysses cross? Hercules? (If you wish, on separate paper, draw pictures of their boats.)

3 On the map of the world below—drawn originally (*c.* 500 B.C.) by the Greek cartographer, Hecataeus—draw arrows showing the probable direction of (1) Ulysses' voyage to the Other World, and (2) Hercules' voyage to Erythia, the island of three-headed Geryon.

The world according to Hecataeus

4 Hecataeus thought of the world not as a sphere but as a disk. Consult the appropriate section of a handbook of Classical mythology, and find the answers to the following questions. If you wish, write out your answers.

What were the early Greek myths about the origin of this supposed world-disk, called Earth? What was imagined as immediately above and below it? In the genealogy of the early Greek gods, what kin was Oceanus to Earth?

15.7 What was Hercules' original name?

Among the brave heroes who sailed across Oceanus was Hercules. Hercules, although he was also known by his Greek name Heracles, had been named at birth by his parents something entirely different.

To find Hercules' original name, first fill each set of blanks with an English word which has come to us from Latin. Then write the numbered letters in the order of their numbers in the space below.

Each word is clued by (1) a related Latin word in parentheses and (2) an English definition.

(claudere) *bring to an end*   __ __ __ __ __ __ __ __

5

(dēlectāre) *give great pleasure*   __ __ __ __ __ __ __

2

(lavāre) *give abundantly*   __ __ __ __ __ __

7

(retinēre) *keep in one's possession*   __ __ __ __ __ __

4

(dictāre) *say something to be written*   __ __ __ __ __ __ __

1

(trahere) *follow the trail of*   __ __ __ __ __

3

(impedīre) *block*   __ __ __ __ __ __

6

Hercules' original name: __ __ __ __ __ __ __

1   2   3   4   5   6   7

Stage 16

16.1 The person(s) who *has/have . . .*
who *had . . .*

In each Latin sentence below, circle the verb-form in parentheses which correctly translates the **boldfaced** English words.

1a *The dancing-girl is dancing in the middle of the dinner which the slaves* **have prepared**
in mediā cēnā, quam servī (parāverant/parāvērunt), saltat saltātrīx.

1b *The dancing-girl was dancing in the middle of the dinner which the slaves* **had prepared**.
in mediā cēnā, quam servī (parāvērunt / parāverant), saltābat saltātrīx.

2a *The young men are watching the dancing-girl, who* **has broken** *out of the large egg.*
iuvenēs saltātrīcem, quae ex ōvō magnō (ērūperat / ērūpit), spectant.

2b *The young men were watching the dancing-girl, who* **had broken** *out of the large egg.*
iuvenēs saltātrīcem, quae ex ōvō magnō (ērūperat / ērūpit), spectābant.

3 *The dancing-girl stretched out her hand and shook the tambourine which she* **had brought** *with her.*
saltātrīx manum extendēbat et tympanum, quod sēcum (tulit / tulerat), agitābat.

4 *The young men, whom the king* **had invited**, *applauded the dancing-girl.*
iuvenēs, quōs rēx (invītāvit / invītāverat), saltātrīcī plaudēbant.

16.2 Vērum aut Falsum?

1 Mark each statement V(*ērum*) or F(*alsum*). If you cannot decide which, leave the blank empty.

_____ 1 decōrum est virīs pavīmenta lavāre.

_____ 2 necesse erat Volūbilī pavīmentum lavāre.

_____ 3 necesse est nōbīs inimīcōs pūnīre.

_____ 4 decōrum erat Belimicō ad Dumnorigem ursam impellere.

_____ 5 decōrum erat Quīntō ursam necāre.

_____ 6 facile est hominī ursam tractāre.

_____ 7 difficile erat ursae Belimicum ferōciter percutere.

_____ 8 facile est iuvenibus ambulāre.

_____ 9 difficile erat Cogidubnō per turbam prōcēdere.

_____ 10 facile erat Cogidubnō per hortum cum Quīntō ambulāre.

_____ 11 facile est dominō vīllās multās possidēre.

_____ 12 commodum erat Quīntō vīllam Pompēiānam retinēre.

2 If you left one or more blanks empty, explain below why you left it or them empty.

16.3 Inscription from Victory Arch

The arch dedicated in A.D. 51 to the Emperor Claudius in commemoration of his victory over the Britons was long ago destroyed. But a large piece of the commemorative inscription from the arch has survived and is shown in the photograph below. (Three other smaller pieces of the inscription (not pictured) have also survived.)

1 Study the photograph:

1 Can you decipher any Latin words? Which?
2 What kind of tools do you think the inscriber used to make the letters in the stone? Do you think paint was applied to the inscribed areas?
3 Did the inscriber use a mix of capital and lower-case letters, or only capitals?
4 How did the inscriber shape the "u"s?
5 How did the inscriber mark the letter meaning "5" so that the reader would know it was a numeral?
6 How did he indicate spaces between words?

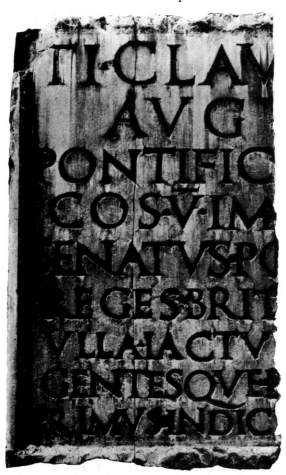

2 Study the translation below, which has been put together from all the pieces, with the addition of some clever guesswork. The English words which translate the Latin (sometimes abbreviated or partly missing) in the large piece shown in the photograph are CAPITALIZED.

> To the Emperor TIBERIUS CLAUDIUS, son of Drusus, Caesar AUGUSTUS Germanicus, PONTIFEX Maximus, holding Tribunician power for the eleventh time, CONSUL for the FIFTH time, saluted as *IMPERATOR* twenty-two times, Censor, Father of his Country.
>   The SENATE and PEOPLE of Rome set this up, because he received the surrender of eleven BRITISH KINGS, who were defeated without ANY LOSS AND because he was the FIRST to bring barbarian PEOPLES on the other side of Ocean under Roman RULE.

3 On a separate sheet of paper, answer the questions below.

1 What was Claudius' personal name? His throne name? (N.B. He inherited the name "Germanicus" from his father.)
2 Which of his titles shows that Claudius was also head of the Roman state religion?
3 How many times had Claudius held the traditional office of *consul*?
4 Who paid for the construction of the arch?
5 What were the two reasons stated for the erection of the victory arch?
6 Find the Latin words (or parts of words) in the photograph which match the capitalized English words in the translation above. Write them out in a double column, labeling one column "English," the other "Latin."
7 In the photograph, find the Latin abbreviations for "TIBERIUS" and "CONSUL." Write them on your paper.
8 In a large Latin dictionary, look up the words "pontifex," "cōnsul," "imperātor," "ūllus/ūlla," "iactūra," "gēns," and "diciō." Write them on your paper along with their meanings. What do you think "pontificī," "sine ūllā iactūrā," and "gentēs" meant in the inscription shown in the photograph? What do you think the "in" of "in diciōnem" meant to the Roman readers? Is the translation above, as "under," incorrect?
9 In the photograph, reread the last line. What might the inscriber have done to make "INDIC(IŌNEM)" easier for the reader to understand?
10 If you wish, draw on construction paper a large facsimile of the stone piece in the photograph. Use the appropriate English words rather than the Latin ones, but write the English words in capitals, using also the inscriber's method of denoting "u"s and spaces between words.
11 If you wish, draw on another sheet of construction paper a large Roman-style victory arch. You will find photographs of the arches in picture-books about the Roman empire, especially in sections showing the Forum of Rome. Or consult Unit 3.

16.4 Bregāns somniat

1 Read the story below and then answer the questions in section 2.

Cervīx in fundō labōrābat. subitō Bregantem, quī in plaustrō
dormiēbat, cōnspexit. Cervīx servum excitāvit et clāmāvit,
    "quam stultus es! perīculōsum est tibi in plaustrō dormīre. Salvius
semper servōs ignāvōs ferōciter pūnit."
    "ēheu!" respondit Bregāns. "ego miserrimus sum, quod dē patre et   5
frātribus meīs somniābam."
    "ubi sunt pater frātrēsque tuī?" rogāvit Cervīx.
    "mortuī sunt," respondit Bregāns. "Rōmānī eōs interfēcērunt."
    tum Cervīcī rem tōtam nārrāvit:
    "ego et familiārēs meī sumus Icēnī. <u>rēgīna</u> nostra erat Boudīca, quam   10
Rōmānī saepe vexābant. tandem Boudīca Icēnōs aliōsque Britannōs
vocāvit et cum Rōmānīs pugnāvērunt. <u>prīmō</u> deī Icēnīs fāvērunt. multōs
Rōmānōs necāvērunt et urbēs Rōmānās dēlēvērunt. Suētōnius Paulīnus,
quī Britanniae praeerat, tandem <u>mīlitēs</u> Rōmānōs <u>contrā Icēnōs</u> dūxit.
Icēnī Rōmānīs fortiter resistēbant, sed Rōmānī eōs superāvērunt. inter   15
mortuōs erant pater frātrēsque meī.
    "post pugnam mīlitēs Rōmānī ad <u>vīcum</u> nostrum vēnērunt, quod
omnēs Icēnōs pūnīre volēbant. virōs fēmināsque necāvērunt et vīcum
dēlēvērunt. mē, quī tum puer eram, nōn necāvērunt sed ad urbem
dūxērunt. vēnālīciō mē vēndidērunt. ēheu! <u>melius erat</u> mihi cum patre   20
frātribusque meīs perīre."
    "quam misera est vīta nostra!" inquit Cervīx. "Rōmānī ferōcissimī
sunt. nōn Britannī, sed Rōmānī sunt barbarī."

somniat: somniāre	*dream*
rēgīna	*queen*
prīmō	*at first*
mīlitēs: mīles	*soldier*
contrā Icēnōs	*against the Iceni*
vīcum:vīcus	*village*
melius erat	*it would have been better*

2 On a separate sheet of paper, answer the following questions.

1 Do you remember Cervix and Bregans from the stories in Unit 2, Stage 13? Who were they? What kind of work did they do for Salvius?

2 Where did Cervix find Bregans? What did Cervix do then?

3 What was Cervix' warning?

4 About whom had Bregans dreamed?

5 Into which native tribe had Bregans been born?

6 Why did the tribal queen Boudica lead an army of Britons in rebellion against the Romans? Was the rebellion successful at first? What did the rebels achieve?

7 Who commanded the Roman army? Was his victory over Boudica and her forces easy? Which Latin word implies the victory took a while?

8 Where did Bregans' father and brothers die? Where do you think his mother died? Why do you think his mother was killed?

9 About how old was Bregans when the Romans sold him into slavery? Do you think he would have been killed if he had been older? Why?

10 Could Salvius have been Bregans' first owner (Boudica's rebellion was put down *c.* A.D. 61.)? Why? About how old would Bregans have been by A.D. 82 when the stories in Unit 2, Stage 13 are imagined to have taken place?

11 Consult a translation of Tacitus, *Annals* XIV.29–39, and write an outline of the major events in the rebellion. According to Tacitus, why was Suetonius Paulinus delayed in putting down the rebellion (XIV.29–30 and 34)? Which legion did he command (XIV.34)? What other soldiers were under his command? In what ways did the Romans mistreat Boudica, her daughters, and other Iceni (XIV.31 and 35)? How many Romans died in the final battle against the rebels (XIV.37)? How many Britons? How did Boudica herself die?

12 On a modern map of Britain, locate the ancient territory of the Iceni tribespeople; it is roughly the same as the modern county of Norfolk. Locate the county of West Sussex, where Salvius' British farm was located. At the time of the Stage 13 stories, about how far was Bregans from his homeland?

16.5 The Palace at Fishbourne

1 Study the picture of the palace. On a separate sheet of paper, state at least **five** different facts about it. Include descriptions of room-use, layout, and decoration. (If it helps you to explain, mark the picture with A, B etc.)

2 Read the four statements below. One is (T)rue, one is (F)alse, and two are (P)ossibly-true. Mark each statement T, F, or P.

_____ A The palace was inhabited by Cogidubnus.

_____ B The palace is very near Cogidubnus' capital.

_____ C The palace was a gift to Cogidubnus from the Romans.

_____ D The palace is not at all Roman in style or layout.

3 Study the floor-mosaics below. (a) is from the palace at Fishbourne, A.D.75, and (b) is from a villa in Pompeii, about the same date. Then follow the instructions at the top of page 39.

(a)

(b)

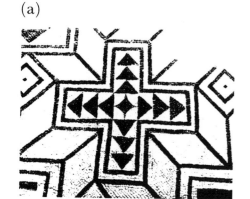

From the evidence you have studied, put a check (✓) in front of the statement which is most likely to be true.

_____ A The same craftsman made both mosaics.

_____ B The owner of the Fishbourne palace liked to imitate the style of high society in Italy.

_____ C All Roman mosaic floors are in a geometric pattern.

4   Below is the ground plan of a large Roman villa excavated in France. Write down

(a) **one** way in which the plan is different from that of the palace at

Fishbourne: _____

_____

(b) **one** way in which it is similar: _____

_____

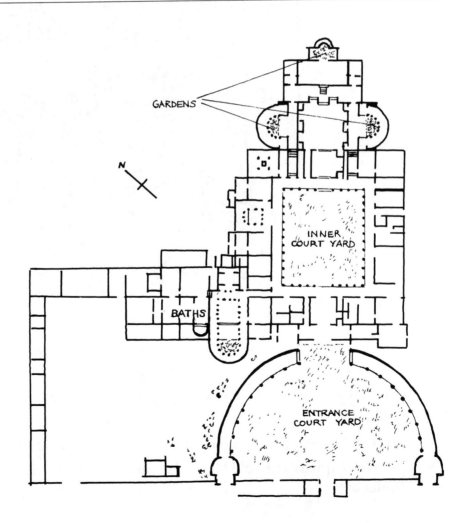

Stage 17

17.1 solēre "to be accustomed, usually"

1 In each Latin sentence below, circle the word in parentheses which correctly translates the **boldfaced** English word(s).

If you wish, first study "sōl," "soleō," and "sōlus" in the complete vocabulary part of the Unit 2 textbook, pp. 199–213.

1 *Many Roman ships **were accustomed** to sailing into the Great Harbor of Alexandria.*

multae nāvēs Rōmānae in magnum portum Alexandrīae nāvigāre (sōlae / solēbant / sōl).

2 *The obelisks which were in front of the Caesareum glittered **in the sun***

obeliscī, quī prō templō Caesaris erant, (solēbant / in sōle / sōlī) fulgēbant.

3 *The lighthouse which stood* **alone** *guarded the harbor.*

   pharus, quī stābat (sōl / solēbat / sōlus), portum custōdiēbat.

4 *Tourists* **usually** *visited the lighthouse island every day.*

   spectātōrēs īnsulam pharī cotīdiē vīsitāre (sōlēs / sōlī / solēbant).

5 *The fire which usually gleamed at the top of the lighthouse was brighter than* **the sun**.

   ignis, quī in summō pharō fulgēre solēbat, splendidior erat quam (sōlus / sōl).

2   Find and label, in the picture opposite, the pharus, the two obelisks in front of the Caesareum, and the Serapeum (temple of Serapis) high on a hill.

17.2 tamen, igitur, *and* enim

Fill the blanks in each English sentence with the best translation of the Latin word in **boldface**.

1   Barbillus magnum gemitum dedit; Plancum **tamen** audīvit.

   Barbillus gave a loud groan; he listened,_____, to Plancus.

2   sacerdōtēs clāmāvērunt, "tacēte vōs omnēs!"; et Plancus **igitur** tacuit.

   The priests shouted, "You all be silent!"; even Plancus,_____, was silent.

3   mīrāculum erat; Plancus **enim** tacēre nōn solēbat.

   It was a miracle;_____ Plancus was not usually silent.

17.3 The Seven Wonders of the Ancient World

1 The Pharos (Lighthouse) at Alexandria was one of the Seven Wonders of the Ancient World. Consult the appropriate section of a reference book or of an ancient history book, and then label each of the remaining six picture-boxes.

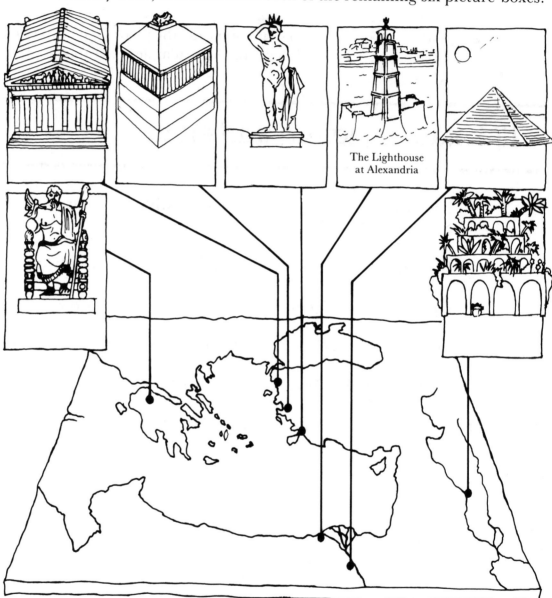

The Lighthouse at Alexandria

2 Research and write an essay in which you describe each of the Seven Wonders pictured above. Describe their size, their manner of construction, and their use or symbolic significance. (You might like to obtain and use as reference the book by Kenneth McLeish, called *The Seven Wonders of the World* (Cambridge University Press 1985).)

Stage 18

18.1 Special Verbs with Dative

1 Fill each blank in the third line with the **dative** form of the noun or pronoun above it. If you wish, first study the charts in the Unit 2 Review Grammar, pp. 162–63 & 172 ¶1.

nominative	ego	tū	custōs	latrō	mīles
genitive	*(not yet learned)*		custōdis	latrōnis	mīlitis
dative	_____	_____	_____	_____	_____

2 Fill each blank with a **dative** form from the line above which translates the English word in **boldface**.

1 *One day a robber came up **to a soldier**.*

latrō _____ quondam appropinquāvit.

2 *After the robber grabbed a rock from the road, he blocked the way **for the soldier**.*

latrō, postquam saxum ē viā rapuit, _____ obstitit.

3 *When a guard arrived he shouted **to the soldier**, "Resist **the robber**!"*

custōs, ubi advēnit, _____ clāmāvit, "resiste_____!"

4 *"I want to resist, believe **me**!" replied the soldier; "but look at the rock in the robber's hand. Side with **me**!"*

"ego resistere volō, crēde _____!" respondit mīles; "spectā tamen in manū latrōnis saxum. favē _____!"

5 *The guard looked at the rock. "I want to side with **you**," he said, "but I must guard the lighthouse." He immediately ran away.*

saxum spectāvit custōs. "ego _____ favēre volō," inquit, "sed necesse est mihi pharum custōdīre." statim effūgit.

6 *"Alas!" said the soldier. "Fortune does not side with **me** today."*

"ēheu!" inquit mīles. "fortūna _____ hodiē nōn favet."

7 *He turned to the robber. "Now," he said, "I put my trust in money, not in the **guard**. Does that please **you**?"*

ad latrōnem sē convertit. "nunc," inquit, "ego pecūniae, nōn _____ cōnfīdō. placetne _____?"

8 *"Yes, it pleases **me**," replied the robber.*

"ita vērō, _____ placet," respondit latrō.

18.2 Quintus and Clemens in Athens

On their voyage from Italy to Egypt, Quintus and Clemens visited Greece and spent several months in Athens.

Read the story and then, on a separate sheet of paper, write the answers to the questions that follow.

Quīntus et Clēmēns, postquam ex urbe Pompēiīs, quam mōns Vesuvius
dēlēverat, effūgērunt, ad Graeciam vēnērunt et in urbe Athēnīs
paulīsper habitābant. per viās urbis saepe ambulābant et multitūdinem
cīvium Graecōrum et servōrum et <u>peregrīnōrum</u> spectāre solēbant.
forum Athēnārum quondam vīsitāvērunt, ubi multī senēs in   5
<u>porticibus</u>, quae forum <u>cingēbant</u>, ambulābant. hī senēs erant
philosophī, quī contrōversiās inter sē cotīdiē habēbant.
"est ūnus deus," inquit philosophus quīdam, "quī nōs amat."
"sunt multī deī," inquit alius, "sed nōs nōn cūrant. nōs hominēs in
terrā sīcut nūbēs in caelō <u>errāmus</u>."   10
Quīntus et Clēmēns, simulatque hōs philosophōs audīvērunt,
effūgērunt.
"ego et tū sumus Rōmānī," dīxit Quīntus. "nōs Rōmānī nōn, sīcut
pīcae in umbrā <u>arboris</u>, <u>garrīmus</u>, sed ad <u>ultimōs</u> fīnēs terrae, sīcut
aquilae, ēvolāmus."   15

peregrīnōrum: peregrīnus	*foreigner, tourist*
porticibus: porticus	*colonnade, portico*
cingēbant: cingere	*surround, ring*
errāmus: errāre	*wander*
arboris: arbor	*tree*
garrīmus: garrīre	*chatter*
ultimōs: ultimus	*farthest*

1 What did Quintus and Clemens do to pass the time in Athens?

2 Whom did they see and hear in the forum?

3 How did they react?

4 Why did Quintus call the Athenians magpies? the Romans eagles?

5 Can you remember any details from the Unit 1, Stage 10 story, "contrōversia," which help explain Quintus' attitude in lines 13–15? If so, what are they?

6 In a handbook of Greek philosophy, research the basic teachings of the Epicureans and of the Stoics. To which of these schools of thought do you think the first speaker (line 8) belonged? The second (lines 9–10)?

7 Consult a book of Greek history or civilization, and look for pictures which will help you identify, in the picture of the Athenian forum (Greek: *agora*), the buildings and places listed below.
Label them in the picture.
1 the acropolis: Erechtheum (temple of Erechtheus), Parthenon (temple of Athena (= Minerva)), Propylaea (monumental entrance)
2 the Areopagus (hill of the High Court)
3 the forum (=agora): odeum (concert hall), stoa (colonnade) of Attalus, temple of Ares (= Mars), stoa of Zeus (= Jupiter), temple of Hephaestus (= Vulcan) and Athena (= Minerva), senate house, prison
4 the Sacred Way

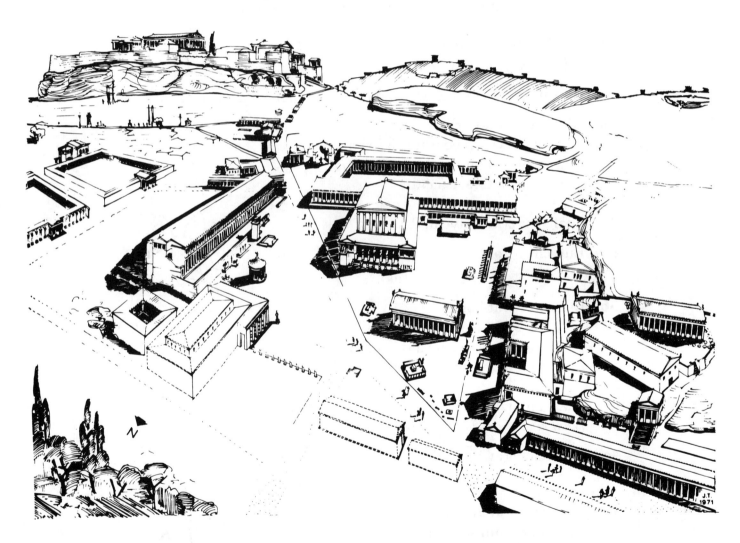

18.3 What kind of person was . . .?

Check (√) the adjectives and relative clauses which correctly answer each question. There may be more than one correct answer in each group.

1   quālis vir erat Barbillus?
What kind of man was Barbillus?

1a Barbillus erat (____ argenteus ____ benignus ____ dīves ____ sacer).

1b Barbillus erat dominus
     ____ quī vīllam ōrnātam habēbat.
     ____ quem operae Aegyptiae pulsāverant.
     ____ quī negōtium cum L. Caeciliō Iūcundō ēgerat.

2   quālis urbs erat Alexandrīa?
What kind of city was Alexandria?

2a Alexandrīa erat (____ exanimāta ____ magna ____ turbulenta).

2b Alexandrīa erat urbs
     ____ quam complēbat turba ingēns.
     ____ quae magnum portum habēbat.
     ____ quae in Graeciā erat.

3   quālis vir erat Eutychus?

3a Eutychus erat (____ benignus ____ īnfirmus
                 ____ īnfestus).

3b Eutychus erat homō
     ____ quī operīs suīs fūstēs dabat.
     ____ quem tabernāriī valdē amābant.
     ____ quī innocentēs laedere temptābat.

4   quāle animal erat haec fēlēs?
What kind of animal was this cat?

4a haec fēlēs erat (____ decōra ____ ferōx
                        ____ sacra ____ sollicita).

4b haec fēlēs erat animal
     ____ quod cum sacerdōtibus Īsidis habitābat.
     ____ quod Clēmēns semper percutiēbat.
     ____ quod caput Eutychī rāserat.

5 quālēs hominēs erant operae Aegyptiae?
What kind of men were the Egyptian thugs?

5a operae Aegyptiae erant (____ bonae ____ crūdēlēs ____ sordidae).

5b operae Aegyptiae erant hominēs
____ quī fēlem sacram floccī nōn faciēbant.
____ quōs Eutychus collēgerat.
____ quī tabernās incenderant.

18.4 What do you see in the picture?

First study the picture below, and then circle the Latin words for the people, the animal, and the objects that appear in the picture.

sella	stola	puella	fēlēs
canis	amphora	Clēmēns	fenestra
Eutychus	fēmina	vitrum	pecūnia
ōlla	manus	pavīmentum	lībertus

18.5 A Glassmaker's Jumble

1 Unscramble the four jumbles below, and form four Latin words.

{ B O R U P U I C }

[P] [ ] [ ] [ ] [ ] [○] [ ] [ ]

{ N I R E B L E T }

[○] [ ] [B] [ ] [ ] [ ] [ ]

{ R O G N A F }

[ ] [ ] [A] [ ] [ ] [○]

{ A S O R B E T }

[ ] [○] [ ] [ ] [ ] [R] [ ]

2 Now write below, in correct order, the letters in the circles, and you will find the English name for an object in the picture.

[○] [○] [○] [○]

3 Describe in your own words what each of the men in the picture above is doing.

48

Stage 19

19.1 Do! Don't!

Check (√) the commands(s) appropriate to the picture.

1 Clemens is talking to Eutychus and his thugs in a bar. He shouts:
   ____ nōlī tabernāriōs terrēre, Eutyche!
   ____ tabernāriōs terrē, Eutyche!

2 Eutychus shouts back:
   ____ nōlī tacēre, Clēmēns!
   ____ tacē, Clēmēns!

3 The thugs shout:
   ____ nōlī dominō nostrō nocēre, Clēmēns!
   ____ nocē dominō nostrō, Clēmēns!

Continued

4 The old man on his back shouts:

_____ pulsāte mē, servī!

_____ nōlīte mē pulsāre, servī!

5 The thugs shout:

_____ nōlī in viā iacēre, amīce!

_____ iacē in viā, caudex!

6 The shopkeeper in the doorway says:

_____ saltā, uxor!

_____ nōlī timēre, uxor!

7 Clemens, who wants to sell the ornamental vase, says:

_____ eme hanc ōllam, domina! pulchrior est.

_____ nōlī hanc ōllam emere, domina! pulchrior est.

8 The lady, who prefers the plain jug, says:

_____ vēnde mihi hanc urnam, tabernārī! ūtilior est.

_____ nōlī mihi hanc urnam vēndere, tabernārī! ūtilior est.

9 The cat, who dislikes being ignored, thinks:

_____ dā mihi cibum, domine!

_____ nōlī mihi cibum dare, domine!

19.2 Who is this? Who are these?

Circle the correct Latin word in parentheses, and then translate the sentences.

1a (haec / hoc / hic) vir est Aristō, quī tragoediās scrībere vult.

1b amīcī (hoc / hanc / hunc) virum numquam vīsitant,
quod semper tragoediās recitat.

2a (hoc / haec / hic) fēmina est Galatēa, uxor Aristōnis.

2b tībīcinēs et citharoedī (hoc / hunc / hanc) fēminam
semper vīsitant, quod cantāre et iocōs facere vult.

3a (hī / hae) puellae corōnās rosārum gerunt.

3b tubicinēs post (hās / hōs) puellās prōcēdunt.

4a (hic / haec / hoc) sacerdōs deae Īsidī sacrificium facit.

4b multī aliī hominēs (hoc / hanc / hunc) sacerdōtem spectant et versūs sacrōs recitant.

5a (hic / hoc / haec) animal est Ariēs (*"animal" is a neuter noun*)

5b vīdistīne (hanc / hunc / hoc) animal? in terrā nōn habitat.

6a (hī / hae) crocodīlī in aquam ruunt.

6b vēnātōrēs (hās / hōs) crocodīlōs interficere volunt.

19.3 Īsis Aegyptia

Isis had been worshiped in Egypt long before the Romans occupied the country. She had also been pictured by native Egyptian artists in a way less natural than the way she was represented by later Greek and Roman artists.

Compare the photograph, in Unit 2, p.125, of a Roman statue of Isis with the copy of an Egyptian drawing of her below.

1 What is the pose of the Egyptian Isis?

 Is her head seen full front or from the side? Her shoulders? Her breast? Her feet? Could a real woman twist herself into this shape?

2 What is the pose of the Roman Isis?

 Is any part of her in the photograph seen from the side? Could a real woman stand like this?

3 The Egyptian Isis is wearing a tight skirt, enfolded by a mantle made of falcon wings.

 What is the Roman Isis wearing?

4 In her right hand, the Egyptian Isis is holding an *ankh*—the Egyptian picture-sign meaning "life"—and in her left hand, a stalk with an open papyrus-blossom. (Papyrus was a sedge-plant which grew in the swamps near the mouths of the Nile river, and from its stems was made the original paper.)

 What is the Roman Isis holding in her hands? What was the purpose of the sistrum? How did it operate? What kind of water are we to imagine she was carrying in the jug?

5 Over her head, the Egyptian Isis is wearing a tight-fitting headdress made from the carcass of a vulture; atop this, set inside a ring of upraised cobras, are the horns of a cow, cradling the sun-disk.

 What is the Greco-Roman Isis wearing over her head? (Perhaps with a magnifying glass you will see the single upraised cobra above the center of her forehead.)

Further Activities

Consult a handbook of Egyptian mythology, and look up in the index the stories about Isis.

1 Describe the quarrel between Isis and Re. (Re was the name of the Egyptian sun-god.)

2 Describe the sufferings of Isis when she lived in the papyrus swamps.

3 Write out versions of these stories in your own words. If you wish, illustrate them with drawings in *your own* style. Is your style more like the Egyptian or the Roman?

19.4 Io, the Human Cow

Read the story below, and then write the answers to the questions that follow.

Īō, vacca hūmāna

Io was a Greek nymph who attracted the attention of the high-god Jupiter. Because his wife Juno was jealous, Jupiter tried to protect Io by turning her into a cow.

Iūppiter Īō, nympham pulcherrimam, in figūram vaccae niveae vertit. Īō īnfēlīx igitur aliquandō, in terrā recumbēns, grāmen frūmentumque dūrum cōnsūmēbat, aliquandō, vix ē terrā surgēns, aquam ē flūmine sordidō bibēbat.

Īō vacca, ubi manūs pedēsque īnspicere temptāvit, ungulās nigrās 5
vīdit. Īō vacca, ubi stolam nitidam īnspicere temptāvit, villōs niveōs vīdit. "ō mē miseram!" sēcum cōgitābat; ubi tamen "ō mē miseram" dīcere temptāvit, cum magnō gemitū mū . . . mūgīvit.

ōlim Īō, postquam patrem Īnachum forte cōnspexit, Īnachō appropinquāvit et eī ōsculum dare temptāvit. 10

"babae! quid agis, vacca?" exclāmāvit pater. "tū es animal valdē molestum! abī, coniunge tē cum cēterīs vaccīs, quae in agrō sunt!"

subitō Īō trīstissimē mūgīvit et, postquam crūs dextrum sustulerat et lentē dēmīserat, ungulam in pulverem firmē impressit et lentē scrībere coepit: 15

I

et deinde difficulter cōnfēcit:

O

"ō mē miserum!" lacrimāvit pater. "tū es Īō, fīlia mea, et quamquam in corpore vaccae habitās mihi cārissima es." 20

But Io's reunion with her father was brief. Jealous Juno sent a gadfly which kept buzzing and biting Io, slowly driving her away from Greece, across land and sea, to Egypt. There, by the banks of the Nile, Io sank down weary, and Jupiter, out of pity, restored her to human shape. The local Egyptians, because they mistook Io for Isis, worshiped her like a goddess.

figūram: figūra	*shape*		Īnachum: Īnachus	*Inachus (King of Argos)*
aliquandō	*sometimes*		crūs	*leg*
grāmen	*grass*		dēmīserat: dēmittere	*lower, let down*
ungulās: ungula	*hoof*		pulverem: pulvis	*dust (cf. English "pulverize")*
villōs: villī	*shaggy hairs*		difficulter	*with difficulty*
mūgīvit: mūgīre	*moo*		corpore: corpus	*body*

1 How did the cow Io pass her time?

2 What did she see when she tried to look at her hands and feet? at her gleaming dress?

3 What happened when she tried to complain?

4 What did she do when she caught sight of her father?

5 How did her father react at first?

6 What did Io do then?

7 How did her father react this second time?

8 Why do you think the Egyptians mistook Io for Isis?

19.5 What do you see in the picture?

First study the picture below and then circle the names of the person and all the objects and rooms which are pictured, either whole or in part.

If you wish, study again the plan of a Pompeian house in Unit 1, Stage 1, p.15. Barbillus' Roman-style house in Alexandria would not have been appreciably different from an elegant house in Pompeii.

peristȳlium	tunica
valvae	culīna
latrīna	pavīmentum
Barbillus	fēlēs
aqua	impluvium
mūrī	larārium
candēlābrum	tablīnum
toga	armārium
triclīnium	Quīntus
stola	statuae
ānulus	ātrium
mēnsa	sella

Stage 20

20.1 The Cut-up Mouse

The astrologer, who thought he was the equal of the doctor Petro, tried to heal Barbillus by cutting up a mouse and placing the tiny pieces in Barbillus' shoulder-wound. (He claimed this remedy had come down from the Chaldaean astrologers of Babylon.) The wound got infected, suppurated, and eventually caused Barbillus' death.

The astrologer, though naive, was correct in attributing the remedy to tradition. The older Pliny, who wrote a Latin encyclopedia called, in English, *The Natural History*, frequently praised the medicinal properties of mice. Mice, or so went the tradition, were lively and life-giving, a piece of mouse was a piece of life.

This faith in the vitalizing qualities of mice was particularly strong in Egypt. When the Nile receded after its flood-peak, mice were suddenly seen everywhere—as the older Pliny noted—jumping around in the mud, and they were thought to have been spontaneously created by the legendary, life-giving water of the Nile.

The desiccated body of an early Egyptian boy, buried in desert soil, preserved in his intestine the remains of his last medicine: "a skinned mouse, young, well chewed, and mixed with vegetables" (G. Majno, *The Healing Hand* (Cambridge, MA: Harvard U.P. 1975), p.138).

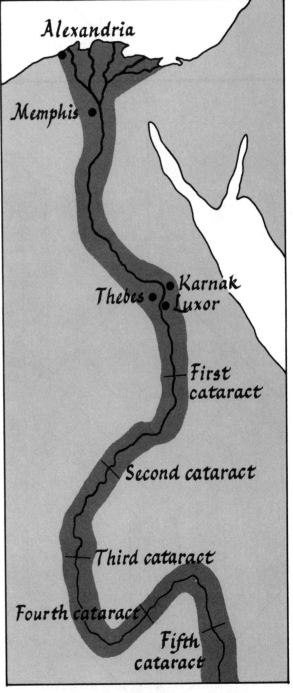

A Project

Consult a history of ancient Egypt, and collect traditions about the Nile. Compose a written or oral report on the superstitions which surrounded this fabled river.

You will find some particularly vivid superstitions in a translation of Book 2 of *The Histories* of Herodotus, an ancient Greek historian.

20.2 Complē hoc pavīmentum!

Geometric mosaics, many of them with hollow-square designs, were popular everywhere in the Roman empire. See, for example, the photograph of mosaics from Fishbourne and Pompeii on page 38.

Fill in the squares of the mosaic opposite with Latin words which translate the English phrases (some hints are provided in parentheses).

All the Latin words have **five letters** each.
Words are to be written **from left to right**, or **top to bottom** (if they are vertical).
Letters in corner squares of adjoining blocks **will match**.

Work out the words on a separate piece of paper, and then match them in the squares.

Block A: s/he is silent
s/he holds
whole (*m., acc.*)
trumpet (*acc.*)

Block B: s/he brought
to/for a friend
crowd
I drag

Block C: safe (*m., acc.*)   (related to English "tutor")
table
everything   (an anagram of "ōmina")
I raise/lift up

Block D: I hurt
chair
I send
alone (*m., acc.*)

Block E: ōmina "omens"
you (s.) dare
oil   (related to English "oleo-")
wall

Block F: bigger, larger
rock
wretched, sad
old man (*acc.*)

Block G: I order
mother
it scratched
he met

Block H: s/he decorates
hatred   (also used as English word)
I was afraid
many (*m.*)

Block I: that (woman) (*acc.*)   (*m.* form in Stage 9 checklist)
with himself/herself   (First half of word is in Stage 13 checklist.)
I have warned
more   (=first 5 letters of Latin word for "foreman" or "teacher")

20.3 Plancus and the Sacred Crocodiles

Read the story below, and then write the answers to the questions.

crocodīlī sacrī

There were many tourist attractions in Egypt, including the sacred crocodiles who lived near Crocodopolis, Crocodile City.

Aristō cum uxōre filiāque <u>in adversum Nīlum</u> nāvigābat. cum eīs ībat
Plancus, vir doctissimus, quī numquam tacēbat. ad urbem Crocodopolim
iter faciēbant, ubi crocodīlōs sacrōs, <u>bēstiās</u> nōtissimās, vīsitāre volēbant.

    in itinere amīcī templum antīquum Sōlis et <u>pȳramidas</u> vīdērunt. hae
rēs mīrābilēs omnēs dēlectāvērunt. Plancum valdē dēlectāvērunt, quod   5
dē monumentīs templīsque <u>garrīre</u> semper volēbat.

    tandem amīcī ad urbem Crocodopolim pervēnērunt. ad <u>lacum</u>
contendērunt ubi sacerdōtēs crocodīlōs sacrōs cūrābant. hī sacerdōtēs,
postquam spectātōrēs in rīpā stantēs vīdērunt, "audīte vōs omnēs"
clāmāvērunt. "nōlīte crocodīlīs appropinquāre! perīculōsum est   10
spectātōribus <u>in extrēmā rīpā</u> stāre."

Feeding time for the crocodiles.

sacerdōtēs crocodīlōs vocāvērunt. crocodīlī statim ad sacerdōtēs
spectātōrēsque <u>natāvērunt</u>. tum sacerdōtēs <u>pānem</u> et <u>carnem</u> et vīnum
in <u>ōra</u> crocodīlōrum posuērunt. postquam crocodīlī cibum   15
cōnsūmpsērunt, sacerdōtēs <u>pannōs</u> cēpērunt et <u>dentēs</u> eōrum lavāre
coepērunt! spectātōrēs <u>fortitūdinem</u> sacerdōtum laudābant. tum
Plancus, quod crocodīlōs <u>propius</u> vidēre volēbat, ad extrēmam rīpam
prōcessit et dē vītā crocodīlōrum garrīre coepit. subitō, prōcumbēns et
garriēns, in lacum inter crocodīlōs cecidit! omnēs <u>commōtī</u> mortem   20
Plancī timēbant. crocodīlī tamen ab eō celerrimē fūgērunt et Aristō
Plancum ex aquā trahere poterat.

    Galatēa, in aurem Helenae <u>susurrāns</u>, "crocodīlī" inquit "Plancum
audīre nōlunt. <u>fēlīciōrēs</u> sunt quam nōs, quī ab eō effugere nōn
possumus."   25

in adversum Nīlum	*up the Nile*	ōra: ōs	*mouth*
bēstiās: bēstia	*wild animal*	pannōs: pannus	*cloth*
pȳramidas: pȳramis	*pyramid*	dentēs: dēns	*tooth*
garrīre	*chatter*	fortitūdinem: fortitūdō	*courage*
lacum: lacus	*lake*	propius	*at closer quarters*
in extrēmā rīpā	*on the edge of the river bank*	commōtī: commōtus	*alarmed*
natāvērunt: natāre	*swim*	susurrāns: susurrāre	*whisper*
pānem: pānis	*bread*	fēlīciōrēs: fēlīx	*lucky*
carnem: carō	*meat*		

1   Which members of Aristo's family were with him?

2   How were they traveling?

3   What two things does the story tell you about Plancus' character?

4   What two sights did the friends see on their journey?

5   Why was Plancus particularly pleased?

6   What was special about the lake to which the friends hurried?

7   What were the spectators doing?

8   What warning did the priests give the spectators, and why?

9   What happened when the priests called the crocodiles?

10   What three things did the crocodiles have for dinner?

11   What did the priests do with the cloths?

12   How did the spectators react to what the priests did (with the cloths)?

13   What did Plancus do then, and why?

14   What happened to Plancus next?

15   How did everyone feel then, and why?

16   What was unexpected about the crocodiles' behavior?

17   Why do you think they behaved this way?

18   What finally happened to Plancus?

19   What was Galatea's explanation for the crocodiles' behavior?

20   In Galatea's opinion, who was luckier than whom, and why?

Published by the Press Syndicate of the University of Cambridge
40 West 20th Street, New York, NY 10011-4211, USA

The Cambridge Latin Course was funded and developed by the
University of Cambridge School Classics Project and SCDC
Publications, London, and is published with the sponsorship of
the School Curriculum Development Committee in London and
the North American Cambridge Classics Project.

© SCDC Publications 1988

First published 1988
Reprinted 1991, 1993, 1994, 1995, 1997, 1998 (twice)

Printed in the United States of America

ISBN 0-521-34856-0

Acknowledgments

I am grateful to the teachers of the Cambridge Latin Course
who have indirectly helped me write this workbook by sharing
with me their classroom worksheets. I am thinking particularly
of the student-teachers in Latin at the University of
Massachusetts at Amherst, and of the American and Canadian
teachers who attended the Cambridge Latin Workshop in
Amherst (1984) and the Cambridge Latin Teachers' Tour of
England (1985).

During the tour of England, I was among the teachers who
visited the lively classes in Classical Studies taught by Ernest
Heatley at Parkside Community College, Cambridge. Stacks of
cartons lined his classroom, every one of them filled with
resource materials and neatly labeled. The wealth in those
cartons is well illustrated by sections 15.2 and 20.2 of this
workbook, since the "plaustrum" and "pavīmentum" puzzles
were originally written by him for his students and appear here
with his permission.

I am also grateful to Richard Woff of the London Institute of
Education for the Latin story about Boudica in section 16.4, to
Pam Perkins of Queen Elizabeth's School for Girls, Barnet for
the exercises in sections 13.5, 14.1, 15.3 and 16.5, and to Pat
Story for exercises in sections 16.4 and 20.3, which were
originally written for British CSCP graded tests and appear here
with permission.

Finally, I am no less grateful to Pat Story, Director of the
Cambridge School Classics Project, for her interest in this
workbook overall and for the many helpful suggestions which
have much improved my original manuscript.

Ed Phinney